Go placidly amid
THE NOISE ANd HASTE

MEDITATIONS ON THE "DESIDERATA"

Go placidly amid THE NOISE ANd HASTE

MEDITATIONS ON THE "DESIDERATA"

BY GRANVILLE T. WALKER

THE BETHANY PRESS

Saint Louis   Missouri

Library of Congress Cataloging in Publication Data

Walker, Granville T
   Go placidly amid the noise and haste.

   Includes bibliographical references.
   1. Christian Church (Disciples of Christ)—Sermons.
2. Sermons, American. I. Title.
BX7327.W28G6   1976   252'.06'3   75-37546
ISBN 0-8272-1217-8

Manufactured in the United States of America

With all becoming grandfatherly pride,
this book is lovingly dedicated to
Mary Chowning
Anne Chowning
Jennifer Walker Chowning
and
Christopher Walker Wilson
Steven Scott Wilson
assured that the message of the Desiderata
will be as needed in their maturer years
as it has been in ours.

FOREWORD

The ministry of Dr. Granville T. Walker has been marked by many notable achievements—as scholar and teacher, as pastor and counselor, as administrator and international leader of the Christian Church (Disciples of Christ). Preeminently, though, he is a preacher of extraordinary skill.

These meditations on the "Desiderata," first presented by Dr. Walker from the pulpit of University Christian Church in Fort Worth, Texas, exemplify his exciting, highly intelligent and spiritually powerful preaching. If the essential nature of a sermon is such to make it impossible for printing to reproduce preaching, as Fosdick once suggested, it is true in Dr. Walker's case only to the extent that the reader is deprived of the forceful impact of his intimate and compelling speaking style.

Always an exponent of intelligent Biblical preaching, Dr. Walker in this unique series uses the obviously restated Biblical ideas from the popular "Desiderata" to proclaim the "essentials" (the meaning of "Desiderata") for human conduct. Ranging from "the passive virtues of humility and peaceable relationships" to "Christian action in meeting the vast and immeasurable needs in our world," there is help here for the reader in making day by day moral and ethical decisions and in finding Christian answers to some of the baffling problems that plague our culture. If the essential purpose of preaching is to enable persons to come to such an insight into their own condition and the condition of their world, that they may be free to live their lives as authentically as Jesus Christ lived His, this is preaching at its best!

Go Placidly amid the Noise and Haste is an excellent companion piece to Dr. Walker's earlier work, **The Greatest of These**, meditations on the thirteenth chapter of First Corinthians published on the occasion of the twentieth anniversary of his service as minister of University Christian Church. The publication of this present volume coincides with the remarkable confluence of four significant events: the centennial celebration of Texas Christian University, the one-hundredth anniversary of University Christian Church, the completion of thirty years by Dr. Walker as pastor of that great congregation, and the announcement of his plan to retire at the end of 1973.

This Foreword provides some opportunity to acknowledge the profound respect and affection held for Dr. Walker by members of the congregation and a grateful brotherhood. Complete objectivity may be too much to have expected in the writing of this Foreword from one so much affected by his preaching, pastoral care and friendship.

Kenneth L. Teegarden
Executive Minister,
Christian Church
(Disciples of Christ) in Texas

PREFACE

Publication of this new edition of my meditations on the "Desiderata" adds something to a number of the relationships that have given direction to my life and ministry over the years.

One of these relationships was with University Christian Church in Forth Worth, Texas, where I served as senior minister for over thirty years. Members of this church first expressed appreciation for these meditations and encouraged me to put them in publishable form.

Another of my relationships has been with Texas Christian University where I have had some official connection, except for two years, since 1932—as student, faculty member, and trustee—and I was deeply gratified when TCU Press published the first edition of these meditations in 1973.

Both University Christian Church and Texas Christian University are now 103 years old. They came into being simultaneously and under the same sponsorship at Thorp Spring, Texas, in the fall of 1873. They were both well established when I first became related to them. Both University and Church enriched me and I cherish the hope that in turn I have been helpful to the people they have served. It was a deeply meaningful experience to share, three years ago, in their respective centennial celebrations.

I have also cherished my relationship to my own denomination—the Christian Church (Disciples of Christ) which has recognized and supported my ministry through the years. I have been honored to serve on a number of its Committees, Commissions and Boards, and during the "Decade of Decision," as Chairman of the Commission on Brotherhood Restructure whose task it was during the eight years of its existence to revamp the loosely organized brotherhood into its present denominational structure.

Dr. Kenneth L. Teegarden, who is now general minister and president of the church, has graciously written the "Foreword" to these meditations.

Through the years, too, I have enjoyed a relationship with the church's publishing unit, the Christian Board of Publication. Articles of mine have appeared in several Christian Board magazines over the years, and its book publishing division, Bethany Press, published two previous books of mine: *The Greatest of These* and *Preaching in the Thought of Alexander Campbell.*

The original publication of this book was made possible by Texas Christian University Press of which Dr. James Newcomer is Director. To him I acknowledge a great debt for his helpful suggestions about form. My appreciation also is extended to Miss Judy Oelfke who designed the book as she has done for many of the works of art in University Christian Church; and to my former secretary, Mrs. Joyce Valentine, who with painstaking care typed and retyped, and proofread the manuscript several times. And for the love and friendship of the fine people who comprise the membership of University Christian Church which Erline and I have served for over thirty years, our gratitude is inexpressible.

Granville T. Walker

January, 1976

TABLE OF CONTENTS

Go placidly amid the noise and haste

After Adlai Stevenson's death in 1965 it was discovered that he had intended to send out as his Christmas card a reprint of the "Desiderata," which is a list of suggestions for human conduct, easily converted into commitments for a new way of life.

The authorship of the "Desiderata" was for a time obscured by the fact that the work appeared in print bearing the legend that it had been discovered on a plaque installed in St. Paul's Church in Baltimore when built in 1692—a claim which caused a bit of controversy and investigation and which was never confirmed. Indeed, there seems to be little question now but that the author of the "Desiderata" was Max Ehrmann, for the work appeared in a book of poems authored by him and published in 1948.

In any event, the "Desiderata" (or "essentials" as the word may be loosely translated) is now a part of American literary lore. Among its virtues is the fact that it restates in fresh and vivid manner ideas that are thoroughly Biblical, but our very familiarity with them dulls the way they strike us. Indeed, there is a remarkable likeness in the "Desiderata" to the sayings and proverbs in the Wisdom Literature of the Old Testament, and to the practical, ethical admonitions which are to be found scattered throughout the writings of Paul.

1

I

Hear then the wisdom of the wise:

"Go placidly amid the noise and the haste, and remember what peace there may be in silence.

"As far as possible, without surrender, be on good terms with all persons. Speak your truth quietly and clearly; and listen to others, even to the dull and the ignorant; they too have their story.

"Avoid loud and aggressive persons; they are vexations to the spirit.

"If you compare yourself with others, you may become vain or bitter, for always there will be greater and lesser persons than yourself.

"Enjoy your achievements as well as your plans.

"Keep interested in your own career, however humble; it is a real possession in the changing fortunes of time.

"Exercise caution in your business affairs, for the world is full of trickery. But let this not blind you to what virtue there is; many persons strive for high ideals, and everywhere life is full of heroism.

"Be yourself. Especially do not feign affection. Neither be cynical about love; for in the face of all aridity and disenchantment, it is as perennial as the grass.

"Take kindly the counsel of the years, gracefully surrendering the things of youth.

"Nurture strength of spirit to shield you in sudden misfortune. But do not distress yourself with dark imaginings. Many fears are born of fatigue and loneliness.

"Beyond a wholesome discipline, be gentle with yourself. You are a child of the universe no less than the trees and the stars; you have a right to be here. And whether or not it is clear to you, no doubt the universe is unfolding as it should.

"Therefore be at peace with God, whatever you conceive Him to be. And whatever your labors and aspirations, in the noisy confusion of life, keep peace in your soul.

"With all its sham, drudgery and broken dreams, it is still a beautiful world. Be cheerful. Strive to be happy."[1]

II

Now out of all these consider only the first:

"Go placidly amid the noise and the haste, and remember what peace there may be in silence," a difficult exhortation to follow, and probably the more important because it is difficult! It would be easier to help make the noise and join in the haste. But if we take this option we are the losers.

One need not be a rebel against the technological achievements of our age to perceive that the noisiness of it, and the speed which has conquered space, have together robbed mankind of something dearly needed and which if possible must be regained. The result is that it is a rare person who knows what silence really is or who, being alone, can manage his solitude! Rarer still are those who have retained in private experience what speed and rush have taken from most others.

A very thoughtful and popular theologian of our time, C.S. Lewis, recalled in his autobiography that it was one of the blessings of his childhood and youth that his family had no modern means of transportation. Most of their friends did. Sometimes these friends would take him for a drive.

"This meant," he said, "that all those distant objects could be visited just enough to clothe them with memories and not impossible desires, while yet they remained ordinarily as inaccessible as the moon. The deadly power of rushing about wherever I pleased had not been given me.

"I measured distances by the standard of man, man walking on his two feet, not by the standard of the internal combustion engine. I had not been allowed to deflower the very idea of distance; in return I possessed 'infinite riches' in what would have been to motorists 'a little room.'

"The truest and most horrible claim made for modern transport is that it annihilates space. It does. It annihilates one of the most glorious gifts we have been given. It is a vile inflation which lowers the value of distance so that a modern boy travels a hundred miles with less sense of liberation and pilgrimage and adventure than his grandfather got from traveling ten."[2]

Fortunately or not, we live in an age in which space is being conquered, not just for astronauts who experience the adventure and the thrill, but for ordinary folk who speed through the park and never see

4

the flowers, who fly from one metropolis to another and never see the mountains. We have lost our ability to measure distances by the standard of a man on his feet. One wonders whether the gain is worth the loss! It might be—if we develop a commensurate competence to move placidly amid the noise and haste and remember the peace there may be in silence.

III

Can we slow the hurried pace? Can we learn now and again to be still and know that God is God?

One has a fellow feeling for J. B. Priestley, who once wrote an essay in his book, **Delight,** on "not going." Said he, "One of the delights known to age and beyond the grasp of youth is that of **Not Going.** When we are young it is almost agony not to go. We feel that we are being left out of life, that the whole wonderful procession is sweeping by, probably forever, while we are weeping or sulking behind bars.

"Not to have an invitation—for the dance, the party, the game, the picnic, the excursion, the gang on holiday—is to be diminished, perhaps kept at midget's height for years. To have an invitation and then not to be able to go — oh, the cursed spite!

"Thus we torment ourselves in the April of our time.

"Now, in my early November not only do I not care the rottenest fig whether I receive an invitation or not, but after I have received it, I can find delight in knowing that I am Not Going.

"I have arrived at this by two stages. At the first, after years of illusion, I finally decided I was missing nothing by not going. Now, at the second, and I hope, final stage, I stay away and no longer care whether I am missing anything or not!"[3]

Of course we cannot live as Priestley suggests, turning away from our fellows with unmeasured gracelessness. But we know what, in essence, he meant. He did mean that whatever the circumstances of a man's life he ought not to allow himself to be pushed around and beleaguered by meaningless demands of one sort or another, that a wise man will slow the hurried pace if it falls within his power to do it. In our rush we miss too much. We are like the woman whose maid, observing her daily mad rush, quietly suggested to her that she was running past more than she was catching up with!

"Go placidly amid the noise and the haste, and remember what peace there may be in silence."

IV

The peace there may be in silence! Peace? But there is much more than peace. For silence is the moment of listening, and no man learns anything while he is talking! But in the silence he learns. He may then hear the call of his fellowman for help. He may then hear God's voice, offering him new courage, new direction, new spirit. But some never give God a chance. They do not go placidly amid the noise and haste.

They are never silent. They rush through life, never stopping to think. They move from one thing to another. Every hour is filled; they are afraid to be alone. The silences of God are never given a chance. So, never relaxed, or quiet or silent, they are never in a mood to receive. It is a way of life which cannot for long be sustained, for they cannot move as fast as everything is moving and they cannot keep the pace. Consequently something takes place which they did not foresee or anticipate.

And then in a moment life itself makes a silence for them. Illness comes. Or grief. Or unexpected failure in what was meant to be a rich enterprise. And the silence is so strange to them. They had never made of it either a friend or a resource, or the occasion of accepting the healing friendship of God! Had they done so, everything might have been different on the side of their own well being. It is a poor way to live in our hurried and noise cluttered world.

V

There is a better way. It is to move placidly amid the noise and haste, and remember the peace there may be in silence. The way is to make room in your life for silence before life makes room for it for you.

This should be for you the hour in which you pray and think, and worship God, and remember in love your fellowman. It should be the hour in which you face your own soul and ask God for the exaltation of His presence within you!

For this cause we gather on the Lord's Day in the Lord's house to be silent, to remember and to pray. It is good to be reminded that the Old Hebrew word for Sabbath comes from a root which means "Stop doing what your are doing!"

But the moratorium on rush and noise thus invoked is for a purpose. The purpose is the soul's renewal. The purpose is to get perspective. The purpose is to get away from the meaningless babble and the destinationless rush.

The purpose is to make it possible to live in the midst of the noise and haste with some degree of serenity. The purpose is to make it possible to hear the still small voice of God and discern the difference between life and death.

In a moment of great depression, the prophet Elijah felt that all was lost. He fled to a place of hiding and waited. A noisy blustering wind disturbed the mountainside but God was not in the wind. An earthquake shook the foundations of his world but God was not in the earthquake. Fire burned in all directions about him but God was not in the fire. Then listening when all had become quiet again, he heard a "still small voice," or as one translation puts it "the sound of gentle stillness," and God was in the silence. He listened and found fresh courage for the venture of life!

Let this, then, be one aim of your life: to go placidly amid the noise and haste, and remember the peace there may be in silence.

NOTES

[1]Max Ehrmann, "Desiderata" (Boston: Crescendo Publishing Co.). © 1927 by Max Ehrmann. All rights reserved. Copyright renewed 1954 by Bertha K. Ehrmann. Reprinted by permission of Crescendo Publishing Co., Boston, Mass.

[2]C. S. Lewis, **Surprised by Joy** (New York: Harcourt, Brace Jovanovich, Inc., 1955), pp. 156-57.

[3]J. B. Priestley, **Delight** (London: Wm. Heinemann Ltd. Publishers, 1951), pp. 136-37. Used by permission.

bE ON GOOd TERMS
withOUT SURRENdER

"Go placidly amid the noise and the haste, and remember what peace there may be in silence." That was first in the list of admonitions. The second in the list sounds very much like a statement from Paul's letter to the Romans, "As far as possible, without surrender, be on good terms with all persons."

I

Paul's statement is so similar one wonders if the writer of the "Desiderata" had not just read the twelfth chapter of Romans before composing his word of advice: "If possible, so far as it depends upon you," says Paul, "live peaceably with all."

There can be little doubt that the duty to "live peaceably" with all, as far as it is possible to do so, is a duty of such an exacting sort that the person does not live who does not at one time or another need help in fulfilling it. And for that reason Paul goes beyond the simple admonition in the "Desiderata" and lays out certain attitudes and ways of conduct which are calculated not to make it easy to live on good terms with others but (excepting only when the situation is completely out of one's hands) to make it possible to do so.

Read through this twelfth chapter of Romans and you can easily discern that all of these aids to peace and harmony are manifestations of the quality of Christian love. Love is, itself, the guiding principle of the Christian community, and one of its distinguishing features is normally a strong impulse toward harmony among all men.

It is the very nature of Christian love to prevent misunderstandings, or at least hold them to a minimum, or, failing that, to rectify them when they do occur, so that they are not permanently hurtful.

The kind of "being on good terms" or the "living in harmony with one another," which the Christian way suggests, is certainly no mere accident. Rather, it is the result of resolutely avoiding the things that endanger it, on the one hand, and, on the other, of positively doing good to those with whom we are brought in contact.

Both aspects of that quality of life which issues in harmony are under consideration in Paul's Roman letter.

II

On the negative side, Paul urgently pleads that the Christian avoid being haughty and arrogant. For however arrogance may manifest itself, whether in "selfish ambition or in the haughty superiority to which it leads," as Dr. Gerald Cragg has put it, "pride destroys the harmony of the community. It also fatally circumscribes the sympathies of anyone who becomes obsessed with his own importance. It cuts him off from association with those who need him, and who might be able to help him in their turn. . . .

"A man of proud spirit . . . will renounce all dealings with those whom he regards as undeserving of his attention, and he will consequently deprive himself both of the joy which comes from helping those who stand in need of his assistance and the unexpected delight that comes from gaining new insights in places where he did not think to acquire them. Wisdom is not confined to those who think they possess it, and often humble folk have much clearer discernment and sharper insight than many who account themselves far better qualified to make pronouncements about the truth."[1]

And this is a point of great importance in the "Desiderata." "As far as possible, without surrender, be on good terms with all persons. Speak your truth quietly and clearly; and listen to others, even to the dull and the ignorant; they too have their story."

They do, indeed, but it is of the very nature of conceit or arrogance to make one unwilling to test his opinions by those of others and certainly never to subordinate his judgment to theirs.

But the man who would, without surrender, be on good terms with others must be always ready to learn. He must avoid that attitude of mind which is the very nemesis of a person of earnest purpose. By his arrogance he may be led to assume that he has nothing to learn and everything to teach. He will find it easy to criticize and to discredit rather than to praise, an attitude which, to say the least, is quite unattractive to the outside observer, especially to one who is trying to estimate the gospel by the performance of its advocates.

III

But, if in seeking to live at peace with others, a man must avoid arrogance and the haughty spirit and condescend to what is lowly, he must also avoid repaying evil with evil. This is a most difficult requirement because when the initiative for a relationship passes out of one's hands, he finds it all too easy to justify a spirit of resentment.

Paul would say, with the backing of what Jesus said about love, that at all costs this attitude must be avoided if possible. In any case, it must not become a settled condition of our human relationships.

There are some sub-Christian levels to which our relationships with other people may descend. One such level is reached when we refuse to do good to those who do no good to us; another is when we are helpful only to those who are helpful to us. Jesus would have regarded either position as the mark of an irreligious man. From His disciples he asked for greater concern for others than either posture would require. If love was, indeed, to be the governing standard of their relationship to others, then to do good only to those who did good to them and to refuse to be helpful to those who were not helpful to them, was to miss the mark of true discipleship. He expected better of his disciples. "What do ye more than others?" was a question which caused them to look deeply within themselves and to their own motives. If the ordinary coin of human discourse is the coin of incivility and unconcern, it is less than Christian, and this was His point.

But the lowest level is the level of vengeance. Aside from the fact that, as Paul says, vengeance

14

belongs to God, when we resort to it we ourselves are conquered by it. Evil can never be conquered by evil. When hatred meets hatred, the dread thing is increased. But when hatred is confronted with love, its only antidote is found. Booker T. Washington once said, "I will not allow any man to make me lower myself by hating him," or, as Abraham Lincoln put it, "The only way to destroy an enemy is to make of him a friend."

IV

"As far as possible, without surrender, be on good terms with all persons," says the "Desiderata." "If possible, so far as it depends upon you, live peaceably with all," says Paul.

Both statements recognize that there may be times when living at peace with others is beyond our control and when the claims of courtesy must give way to the claims of principle. Our Christian faith does not require that we shut our eyes and submit with an easy-going tolerance to everything that happens. On the contrary, there may come times when we cannot escape a genuine battle between right and wrong, and no true Christian will shirk his responsibility in such situations. We can live at peace with others only insofar as we can control the situation. We must resist or surrender.

Paul knew, as we surely do, that there are persons for whom living peaceably with their fellows is more difficult than it is for others, that some have controlled more temper than others may even possess! In like manner, it is easier for some, by nature, to be "good" than it is for others. Knowing this, it should be easier for those who are fortunate in this regard to avoid criticizing and judging those who were not endowed by nature so well. And, with such knowledge, the less fortunate may also find their discouragement softened.

But when things have not passed out of our hands and we have avoided arrogance on the one hand and vengeance on the other, we are still under orders to do positive good even to those who would do us harm.

It is of the essence of Christian conduct that the Christian will bless those who curse him. In the very process he will seek their good, pray for their well-being and do his utmost to answer his own prayer!

The Christian does not return evil for evil; rather, he overcomes evil with good. He prays for those who persecute him. It was Plato who said that a good man will prefer to suffer evil rather than to do evil. And it is always evil to hate.

The great example of this positive response to evil is in both the teaching and in the life of Christ. When reviled, He reviled not again. When nailed to the cross, He prayed for those who were executing Him. And He set the example followed by His disciples. Stephen prayed for his persecutors as they stoned him to death. In all of history there has been no greater spiritual force than this serene forgiveness characterized by Christians who, when in the worst of situations, were the best followers of their Lord.

Consenting to the act and holding the coats of those who were killing Stephen was Saul of Tarsus. No scholar doubts that this episode was an important factor in turning Saul of Tarsus into Paul the obedient servant of the Lord Jesus Christ. St. Augustine wrote,

"The Church owes Paul to the prayer of Stephen."

It was this remarkable spirit in the disciples in the early church which gave them such influence that they were accused of turning the world upside down. That was precisely what they were doing. They were behaving according to standards which were a complete reversal of the standards of the world about them.

When their enemies hungered, they fed them. When they were thirsty, they gave them to drink. When they blessed, whether friends or enemies, their blessing was not mere words. It included deeds performed, acts of helpfulness in return for acts of hurt. They had no illusions about what it means to bless and curse not. You do not bless a hungry man, whether he is good or not, whether he deserves it or not, until you feed him. You bless a thirsty man by giving him a cup of cold water. The disciples never forgot the practical truth that "spiritual fare is poor sustenance for an empty stomach." This is why the program of help in the Great Hour of Sharing is so vastly important. If through it we are able to help the helpless help themselves, then genuine blessing will have occurred and with it the kind of reconciliation of man with man and man with God which reflects the true mission of Christ's church.

V

"As far as possible, without surrender, be on good terms with all persons." You do not surrender your highest principles to do this. In dealing with those who do no good to you, you do good to them. And, in dealing with those you love, you do the same, with the added joy of being able to rejoice when they rejoice and weep with those who weep.

Thus, you are not overcome by evil, but you overcome evil with good.

NOTES

[1]**Interpreter's Bible,** IX, p. 593. Copyright 1954 by Pierce and Washabaugh (Abingdon Press).

speak your truth quietly, and listen

The "Desiderata" is a wise man's list of suggestions for human conduct—a list which must unquestionably have been inspired by the author's knowledge of truths that are common to much Biblical literature, especially the ethical and practical admonitions to be found in the letters of Paul and in the Wisdom Literature of the Old Testament.

"Go placidly amid the noise and the haste, and remember what peace there may be in silence. As far as possible, without surrender, be on good terms with all persons."

This admonition is certainly of such an exacting sort that any person needs help in fulfilling it. In the last chapter we were discussing how Paul, in an almost identical statement, laid down certain suggestions about how this might be done. To live at peace with others without surrender certainly requires, as Paul saw so clearly, that one avoid being arrogant and vengeful, but that rather, in dealing even with one's enemies, he should return good for evil, which is the only way evil ultimately can be conquered.

The "Desiderata" also has some suggestions for being able to live a peaceful life in the midst of the noise and haste and for living on good terms with others without surrender.

I

One such admonition is that we deal gently with others and learn to listen when they speak. To do so does not mean that the Christian man is a man without convictions of his own, but it does mean that you are to "Speak your truth quietly and clearly; and listen to others, even to the dull and the ignorant; they too have their story."

To speak one's truth quietly and clearly calls for considerable restraint on the part of a man of deep convictions, but not to do this is to be vexing to others.

It is not easy to like an opinionated person, even when his opinions are right. So, as the "Desiderata" states it, one is to "Avoid loud and aggressive persons; they are vexations to the spirit." But, more than avoiding them, we must make sure we are not the very kind of person we are trying to avoid!

If we proclaim a positive opinion without being sure of our facts, we may have to modify it with much embarrassment.

Some people with strong convictions can voice them without annoyance, but others let their convictions build walls of alienation and disgust by the haughty confidence with which they express them. Some are always the "devil's advocate" in espousing the opposite side on almost any issue, and, frequently, those who hold strong opinions find it difficult to believe that they can ever be wrong. These are the people in any "town meeting" who draw fire from an opposition that takes great delight in exposing their errors. Because we all make mistakes, none of us can afford the luxury of the over-confidence and self-assurance which rules out the possibility of being wrong. If we maintain an attitude of openness, our positions may be accepted with less resistance when we are right, and we can retreat with less embarrassment when we are wrong.

Therefore it is a wise course to speak your truth as you see it, quietly and clearly, and listen to others. Even the best informed people must be prepared to modify their opinions when they are in disagreement with a demonstrated fact. To do this is to experience a wholesome kind of repentance.

And yet it is possible to be too agreeable, so much so that one really has no convictions. A man who does not have convictions and is not prepared to defend them is not worth listening to. There is error in both directions. The too-agreeable are not heard; the overly-opinionated invite resistance and resentment. Says the Book of Proverbs: "Do you see a man who is wise in his own eyes? There is more hope for a fool than for him."[1]

So the truly wise man will speak his truth quietly and clearly and listen to others, even the dull and ignorant; and he will experience the unexpected delight that comes from gaining new insights in places where he did not think to acquire them. Wisdom is not confined to those who think they possess it. Often the humble folk have it too, but they possess it without offense. Speak your truth quietly and clearly, and listen!

II

The "Desiderata" gives still another suggestion for the inner life of peace, and that has to do with the measure we use when we begin to estimate ourselves.

"If you compare yourself with others, you may become vain or bitter, for always there will be greater and lesser persons than yourself." We must listen to others, but it is poor business to be always comparing ourselves with them. For if we do, we may find envy and bitterness overtaking us as we see others better circumstanced than ourselves; or we may become vain and entertain feelings of superiority when we compare ourselves with those less fortunate than we.

If a man sincerely desires to escape both bitterness and vanity, his best way is not to compare himself with others but so learn to identify himself with them that he will be able to rejoice when they rejoice and weep when they weep.

This is not easy to do, but such identification is almost essential to the avoidance of vanity and bitterness and the achievement, in their stead, of a genuine quality of humility.

Many a person has envied his neighbor, thinking that he has an easy time of it, when the truth may well be that the envious person never really has seen the inside problems of the other person's life. It is not easy to know the difficulties of another man's job unless we have actually worked at his kind of work. If we have not employed other people, it is difficult to appreciate the pressure of meeting a payroll.

On the other side, if we never have worked for less than a living wage, if we have never been unemployed or faced the grim fact of actual need, we would not find it easy to sympathize with those placed in such situations. Those who have never been ill, or hurt, or hungry, who have never experienced sorrow or great disappointment, must have real depth of compassion to appreciate fully the feelings of people who have gone through these adversities.

In any event, if we really knew, from the inside, the other fellow's true situation, it is doubtful we would want to trade places with him.

There is a story of the man who came to the place where all men bring their burdens, in the hope of exchanging his load for that of someone else. But after looking at the trouble of others, he was willing to take up his own again! As the years go along we come to learn that all men have their full share of troubles, and that, by comparison, some of our own seem much less heavy. When all the facts are known, it is highly probable that folk we may once have envied or thought were troublefree are carrying around in their lives and in their hearts many things that we wouldn't wish to take on, not even if in doing so we could lay down our own load. We do learn, somehow, to live with our own troubles, but it probably would be very difficult to learn to live with someone else's load.

No, we escape vanity on the one hand and bitterness on the other, not by comparing ourselves with others who may be more or less fortunate than ourselves, but by identifying with them in the profoundest possible sense.

III

It may not be easy to see, but bitterness and vanity (or envy) are conquered ultimately by the love which is the undiscourageable goodwill and compassion which we extend to others, and by genuine humility which is a quality of spirit existing when we have made a true estimate of ourselves. The true estimate does not come from comparing ourselves with others, but by comparing ourselves with the perfect standard of Christ, who stands ever ready to help us bridge the gap between what we are and what we ought to be.

William Sullivan once wrote that genuine humility does not arise from the sense of our pitiable kinship with the dust that is unworthy of us, but from the realization of our awful nearness to a magnificence of which we are not worthy!

James Barrie put it in another way: "The life of every man is a diary," he said, "in which he means to write one story and writes another; and his humblest hour is when he compares the volume as it is with what he vowed to make it."

There, indeed, is the only true comparison: the standard up to which we committed ourselves to live, as against the degree to which we have fulfilled it!

This comparison is what leads to the recommitment of a man's life to all that is good and true and holy.

Far from making him envious of another who is more fortunate than he, or vain because he is himself better than others, it makes him humble. For he now knows what he ought to be and what his resources are in Christ for achieving his goal. That could be one of the truly important moments in a man's life. It could be the place where he acknowledges his need and where, by the grace of God, the need is met.

"Go placidly amid the noise and the haste, and remember what peace there may be in silence. As far as possible, without surrender, be on good terms with all persons. Speak your truth quietly and clearly; and listen to others, even to the dull and the ignorant; they too have their story. Avoid loud and aggressive persons; they are vexations to the spirit. If you compare yourself with others, you may become vain or bitter, for always there will be greater and lesser persons than yourself."

NOTE

[1]Proverbs 26:12.

ENJOY
YOUR ACHIEVEMENTS

"Enjoy your achievements as well as your plans. Keep interested in your own career, however humble; it is a real possession in the changing fortunes of time. Exercise caution in your business affairs, for the world is full of trickery. But let this not blind you to what virtue there is; many persons strive for high ideals, and everywhere life is full of heroism."

The "Desiderata" is concerned with a way of life which if followed will enable a person to go placidly amid the noise and the haste and to remember the peace there may be in silence.

One step of that way is to be on good terms with all persons, if this can be done without surrender. Another step is to speak your own truth quietly and clearly, but listen to others, even the dull and ignorant for they too have their story. In the process, you will avoid loud and arrogant persons who are a vexation to the spirit, but you will also avoid being the very kind of person you are trying to avoid.

Still another step is always to keep an honest estimate of yourself and avoid bitterness and vanity by not comparing yourself with others whose real situation you cannot fully understand because you cannot fully know what it is.

Then the wise author of the "Desiderata" comes to deal with that portion of a man's life which consumes most of his time from birth to death—his work, his career, and his relationship to other people in the world where his vocation is fulfilled, whether in business, or a profession, or a craft.

Says he, "Enjoy your achievements as well as your plans. Keep interested in your own career, however humble; it is a real possession in the changing fortunes of time."

I

Enjoy your achievements as well as your plans!

One would suppose it to be a rather common practice to focus most of our pleasure on setting goals and making the trip, rather than the joy of actually arriving. Robert Browning must have had such a thought in mind when he wrote:

"Ah, but a man's reach should exceed his grasp,

Or what's a heaven for?"("Andrea del Sarto")

It is an unsatisfied hunger to achieve which spurs us on, but once having arrived we have no peace until we have chosen a new destination and have begun to move again.

Take almost any area of human endeavor which has succeeded in this century and you will see without much argument that this is so. In 1903 the Wright Brothers flew the first airplane. Fourteen years later aircraft factories were in operation and the first planes flew in World War I. Unsatisfied with such meager beginnings, in 1927 Charles A. Lindbergh flew the Atlantic, as much a pioneer in aviation as the astronauts have been in space. He was the first man to cross the ocean, non-stop, in a plane.

Now 20,000 people cross it daily in jets. Unsatisfied even with that tremendous accomplishment we have put men on the moon, and it is not unthinkable that within the lifetime of some people now living interplanetary travel will be common, that even hospitals will be aloft in space.

Free of the pull of gravity it is possible, says Edward Lindaman, that "A rest home in space could be a permanent haven for the crippled and infirm, since they would no longer need crutches or wheelchairs. They could dive, float, sail and roll languorously at will, and move from place to place with a finger tip push. Their lives could be far more self-reliant and useful than on Earth . . . .

"An orbital hotel, with variable gravity suites and possibilities for exhilarating new kinds of recreation was seriously discussed at a 1967 symposium on 'Commercial Uses of Space.' "[1]

At this moment there are several hundred satellites orbiting the earth sending back reports which reasonably could change the whole life of mankind on this planet: discerning the location of additional resources we have not yet discovered, reading the weather for long periods in advance, warning of coming floods sufficiently early to save hundreds of lives and countless millions of dollars in houses and buildings, serving as relay stations for worldwide television and radio broadcasts so that we can see and hear in a matter of seconds what is happening on the other side of this planet.

This has been, despite the terrible social problems of racism, of overpopulation threats, and the pollution of our natural resources, a great time in which to live.

II

One of the virtues of this period is that those who have had the remarkable privilege of being involved in these accomplishments have enjoyed moment by moment what was going on. It really is the only way to live. Following the ancient admonition, "Whatsoever thy hand findeth to do, do it with thy might," scientists and workmen have felt themselves a part of something vastly greater than themselves, in itself a deeply religious mood.

For to be religious, in the profoundest sense, is to have the feeling that what you are doing has meaning and significance, not only to yourself, but to others; and, in the area just cited, that significance may be for all mankind for all time to come. It is then that your personal religion is relevant. It is then that you can give yourself completely to the task at hand.

On Arturo Toscanini's 80th birthday someone asked his son, Walter, what his father ranked as his most important achievement. The son replied, "For him there can be no such thing. Whatever he happens to be doing at the moment is the biggest thing in his life—whether it is conducting a symphony or peeling an orange!" Well, no religion is irrelevant if it helps people to see the hidden glory of the common things they do as well as the uncommon things which may represent their greatest achievements as the world measures their work.

III

Here, too, is a clue to at least one major secret of happiness; for, as Aristotle long ago taught, happiness comes chiefly by some productive act, a working in the way of excellence. "Our happiest moments," says Elton Trueblood, "are not those in which we ask how to be happy, but rather those in which we so lose ourselves in some creative task, which seems to us important, that we forget to take our own emotional pulse. When we plant trees, write books, build houses, or make roads, we often find that we have been having a wonderfully good time and that we are not immediately driven to do something to have fun. We have had, all along, something better than anything which commercialized and self-conscious entertainment can ever provide."[2]

IV

Behind the massive youth drop-out in our culture one of the factors may be that work as they have witnessed it in the life of the older generations has become meaningless. They have observed that for many the only real satisfactions in life have come not from their work by which they have made their money, but from the empty gratification they have received only from the spending of money!

The really fortunate people in our culture are those whose work has become their pleasure. James Barrie once said that nothing is really work unless you would rather be doing something else! Work which offers no pleasure is work indeed. But work which it is a joy to do, work which is regarded as sacred to the worker because he believes this is God's world and anything he does to improve man's life is within the limits of God's plan, that is the work for which the pain of drudgery has been made endurable and to which the joy of relevance has been added. If this is truly God's world, then, as Trueblood has said, any true work for the improvement of man's life is a sacred task and should be undertaken with that fact in mind.[3]

Henry David Thoreau once asked an Irishman how many potatoes he could dig in a day and was well pleased with the reply: "Well, I don't keep any account. I scratch away, and let the day's work praise itself."

That surely is a Christian view of a menial task, for the day's work cannot finally praise itself unless it has been rendered in service to mankind. Some do not reach that pinnacle. They work to eat and eat to live and live to eat, and so on. They wind up like Sam whose boss recently discharged him. "Where's Sam?" asked an acquaintance. "Sam doesn't work here any more," came the reply. "Do you have someone in mind for his vacancy?" To which the answer came, "Pshaw, when Sam left he didn't leave no vacancy." Poor Sam, he could enjoy neither his achievements nor his plans!

V

You can enjoy your achievements as well as your plans if you are able, when the day is done, or the task accomplished, to affirm that because it served mankind there is dignity in what you have done. You will have a sense of glory in it because you have regarded your work as having a sacramental significance. Without that, no good work will continue. If on a wide scale a negative view of work were felt, our civilization would cease to advance. As Alfred North Whitehead observed, "A civilization which ceases to advance is already in full decay, because advance and decay are the only choices open to mankind."

With the "sense of glory" and the "feeling of dignity" in a finished task you can enjoy it and have a right to enjoy it. Helen Keller's biography of Anne Sullivan Macy, her teacher whom you saw portrayed in "The Miracle Worker,"recounts the fact that it was without regret that Anne Sullivan left the world on October 20, 1936. A few weeks before the end one who meant to comfort said, "Teacher, you must get well. Without you Helen would be nothing." "That would mean," Anne Sullivan replied sadly, "that I had failed." For her basic aim had always been to make Helen free—even of her. But there was no sadness,

33

only the joy of accomplishment, for the teacher had not failed.[4] Though she had given her entire adult life for only one person, Helen Keller, she could look back with pride that her pupil, blind and deaf and dumb when she began her work, was now as complete a person as one who lived with sight and hearing and voice.

VI

The line between one's plans and one's accomplishments can be drawn only when the job is done, but, even then, for the man who continues his labors in some creative form, planning and achieving really become one.

This is why the author of the "Desiderata" added one more word: "Keep interested in your own career, however humble; it is a real possession in the changing fortunes of time."

It was Jesus who said, "My father worketh hitherto and I work. We must work the works of him who has sent me while it is day for the night cometh when no man can work."

And Thomas Carlyle had a word for it: "Blessed is he who has found his work; let him ask no other blessedness."

"Keep interested in your own career however humble; it is a real possession in the changing fortunes of time." It is, indeed. But that does not mean that a man must do the same old thing in the same old way in the same old place. To keep interested may require movement—new situations, new faces, new people to deal with, new problems to tackle. This is only so one can have the real joy of both his plans and his achievements.

On the tombstone of the novelist, Winifred Holtby, are inscribed these words:

> God give me work
> Till my life shall end
> And life
> Till my work is done.

Cardinal Newman, in a prayer with which he ended a sermon in the mid-1800's, summed it all up in an ardent supplication:

"O Lord, support us all the day long of our troublous life, until the shadows lengthen and the evening comes, and the busy world is hushed and the fever of life is over and our work is done. Then in thy great mercy grant us a safe lodging and a holy rest and peace at last. Amen."

NOTES

[1] Edward Lindaman, **Space, A New Direction for Mankind** (New York: Harper and Brothers, 1969), p. 125.

[2] Elton Trueblood, **The Common Ventures of Life** (New York: Harper and Brothers, 1949), p. 93.

[3] **Ibid.,** p. 85.

[4] From **Teacher** by Helen Keller © 1955 by Helen Keller, (New York: Doubleday & Co. Inc.)

bE NOT bliNd
TO WHAT ViRTUE ThERE iS

"Exercise caution in your business affairs, for the world is full of trickery. But let this not blind you to what virtue there is; many persons strive for high ideals, and everywhere life is full of heroism."

While most of the "Desiderata" deals with the passive virtues of humility and peaceable relationships, a portion of the wise man's sayings is devoted to those disciplines of selfhood which have to do with daily work: "Enjoy your achievements as well as your plans. Keep interested in your own career, however humble; it is a real possession in the changing fortunes of time. Exercise caution in your business affairs, for the world is full of trickery. But let this not blind you to what virtue there is; many persons strive for high ideals, and everywhere life is full of heroism."

That admonition can be summed up in the simple statement: Be careful but not cynical!

The two approaches balance each other, and each needs the other for completion.

One does need to be cautious in dealing with others, for the world is indeed full of trickery. But one may become so careful of getting hurt, or cautious of being "taken," as to go through life suspicious of nearly everyone he meets.

Somehow a man must learn to exercise

reasonable caution on the one hand and reasonable trust in his fellow man on the other if he is to "remember what peace" comes from wholesome human relationships. Few qualities are more calculated to rob a person of genuine happiness than the quality of being suspicious of others, of feeling that everybody has "an angle." It is better to trust and be deceived than never to trust at all.

I

The world is full of trickery, but let this not blind you to what virtue there is.

Many are blinded to what virtue there is, that many persons strive for high ideals and that everywhere life is full of heroism.

Their blindness results in distrust, in suspicion, and, indeed, in cynicism.

Could it be that Raymond Massey was right when he said that most of our suspicions of others are aroused by our knowledge of ourselves? Is it our knowledge of ourselves, unconscious but nevertheless real and definitive of our attitudes toward others, which causes us to live with a sense of distrust?

We do not believe in the heroism of others because we have serious questions about our own. We do not fully trust the idealistic commitment of others because our own commitment is weak and flabby. So, we project our weaknesses, the things about ourselves which we most despise in others. We project these weaknesses on to other people and then hold them in suspicion!

II

It is a fact that we tend to wear masks to hide our real selves from others so that they will think more highly of us than we deserve, and to keep ourselves from acknowledging the truth about ourselves. This causes us to discount the fact that many strive for high ideals and that everywhere life is full of heroism.

Let us explore this fact about ourselves for a moment. By reason of our animal nature we enter life with organic hungers and biological urges, with capacities for lust and fear, rage and hate. Often we find it difficult to hold these native drives in check. Frequently we are ashamed of them; sometimes we are embarrassed by them. But on the other side of our native equipment are hopes and dreams, godlike powers, aspirations after goodness and brotherliness, and fellowship with God which often we find it difficult to achieve.

These contending forces are at work in each of us, but we want to present ourselves to the world at our best and not our worst. Indeed, we want to be our best, and we want to have a high opinion of ourselves. The self-image as well as the image we wish to project toward the world is important to our sense of identity. So we wear masks to make sure that others think more highly of us than we deserve and to disguise our baser impulses from ourselves. Our true destiny, of course, is not found in wearing these masks but in achieving the real spiritual potential which is ours as children of God.

Yet we wear the masks. And we wear them not because we are all bad, but because above all we want to be good. Nevertheless with the masks we tend to deceive ourselves more than the world outside. In turn, because unconsciously we know we wear them, we assume that all others do so, too, and this blinds us to what virtue there is, the high ideals and the inspiring heroism with which life is full.

III

It is important that we should come to know our real selves, that we should really and honestly understand ourselves with all the masks removed if we are going to learn the first principles of trusting others and of running the risk of that trust!

There are several ways by which such self-understanding can be brought about. Some people are so self-deceived that only in-depth study by a trained scientist of the human mind can unearth their disguises. Although most people are not abnormal, all of us, to some extent, go through life self-deceived. In any event let me propose a review of some questions advanced by Richard L. Evans under the title "Self-searching," which was his effort to get the common run of us to look honestly at ourselves.[1]

Perhaps as we probe these questions we may for the moment trade our masks for mirrors and see ourselves as we actually are, an exercise which may start us on the way of becoming what we ought to be. Here are the questions as they appeared in a little book by Richard Evans:

"If you were choosing someone you had to trust, could you trust yourself?

"Would you like to meet yourself when you are in trouble?

"Would you like to be at your own mercy?

"If other men did not put locks on their homes, on their barns, and on their banks, would you ever walk in where you knew you had no right to walk?

"If there were no accounts, no bonding companies, no courts, no jails, no disgrace—none of the usual fears except your own soul inside of you—would you ever take what you knew you had no right to take?

"Would you serve a man without influence as fairly as you would a man with influence?

"Would you honor an unwritten agreement as honestly as if it were written?

"If you found a lost article that no one else could possibly know you found, would you try to return it or would you put it in your own pocket?

"Would you stay with your principles no matter what price you were proffered for forsaking them?

"Would you compromise on a question of right or wrong?

"Do you talk as well of your friends when they aren't around as when they are?

"If you make a mistake, would you admit it or would you pretend to be right even when you knew you were wrong?

"Could you be trusted as well away from home as you could where you are known?

"Do you think the world owes you a living or do you honestly know that you should work for what you want?

"Do you make an earnest effort to improve your performance or have you been hoping for an undeserved improvement in your pay or your position?

"Do you try to get the job done or have you been loafing along for fear you were doing too much?

"Would you hire yourself? Would you like to work for yourself?

"If you were your own partner, could you trust yourself?

"If your partner were to die, would you treat his family as fairly as if he were alive?

"If he lost his health, would you still deal with him not only justly but generously?"

Well, that's a tough list! But there are times when in order to become what we ought to be, we need to know and understand ourselves as we are. Indeed, if we are convinced that the world is mostly filled with trickery so that we discount the heroism and idealism and the virtue that are everywhere, could it not be that our suspicions are rooted in an unadmitted awareness of our own moral turpitudes and weaknesses?

IV

Of course that is not the whole story. But it might just give us an insight into how we appear at least at times to other people. Dr. Leiper tells the true story of an American gentleman who was taking the channel steamer from Fusan in Korea to Nagasaki. This happened quite a while ago, before World War II. The American found himself sharing a stateroom with an Oriental gentleman. After the steamer had left port the American went to the purser and said, "I don't like the looks of that Jap in my stateroom. I want you to put my valuables in your safe." "All right, sir," said the purser, "he brought his down about half an hour ago!" It could be that they were both wrong in their misgivings about each other, but if both learned what had gone on both might have discovered how they appeared in each other's eyes.

Such self-knowledge is the beginning of wisdom. But of course the negative side is not all of it.

For the other side of it is that we are possessed of godlike powers, hopes and dreams, aspirations after goodness and brotherliness and fellowship with God, and we deeply want to be our best. Moreover, most other people are like that, too, a fact about both them and ourselves which we do not often enough allow for.

Perhaps our problem is that we do not care to see these qualities in others because to do so is to admit that there are those who are better than ourselves. If we do not look for these virtues in them, they will in all likelihood not look for them in us.

V

We do not need to pretend to be other than we are when we trade our masks for mirrors and see there not only our evil inclinations but our good as well.

The truth is that Jeremiah was right when he said that the heart is deceitful above all things and dreadfully wicked. But Jesus also was right when He said that the good man out of the good treasure of his heart brings forth that which is good.

For love and goodness and hope are there as well, and every man's foremost problem is to see himself as he actually is—faults and virtues together—and then determine what he shall do with his life.

When we remove the masks and look in clear mirrors, we are on the way to becoming what we ought to be. Within us all there are possibilities for strength and potentialities for good which we never have developed fully, and which some of us never have recognized as being there at all.

When we see them and determine to live up to our full stature, we shall learn to trust ourselves first of all. Beginning there, we will not let the trickery which we know to be in the world blind us to what virtue there is.

Many persons put the weight of their lives on the side of the good and strive for high ideals. Everywhere there are those who face life's misfortunes with unconquerable courage, inspiring the rest

44

of us when we are tempted to be cowards and run away, and everywhere life is full of heroism.

NOTE

[1]Richard L. Evans, **Tonic for Our Times** (New York: Harper and Brothers, 1952), pp. 19-20.

bE youRsElf

"Exercise caution in your business affairs, for the world is full of trickery. But let this not blind you to what virtue there is; many persons strive for high ideals, and everywhere life is full of heroism.

"Be yourself. Especially do not feign affection. Neither be cynical about love; for in the face of all aridity and disenchantment, it is as perennial as the grass."

It would not be a difficult undertaking to prove that one of the major preoccupations of large segments of our culture is with such questions as "Who am I?" If we start with the admonition from the "Desiderata" to "Be yourself," then the question is "What self?"

The emergence in the past few years of sensitivity training, whereby persons examine their own deep emotional responses to life in an effort to come to understand themselves and their own drives and urges more fully, is certainly one indication of this preoccupation with one's selfhood.

There are phrases which have come into the current vernacular which also signal this concern: such as, that a person ought to "do his own thing," that one ought to "tell it like it is," or that this or that type of involvement either is or is not "my bag."

Many of the youthful drop-outs in our culture

justify their way of life on the ground that they are searching for their own true selves, and even those who indulge in the use of hallucinogenic or other types of drugs do so claiming that they are, by this experience, achieving a deeper awareness of themselves. Rarely has so important an issue had to bear the burden of so many questionable forms of the human search or been used as a means of rationalizing behavior which in previous generations has been regarded as open to highly adverse moral judgment.

I

When we come to deal with the simple admonition "Be yourself," it turns out not to be so simple. For in order to "be" ourselves, we need first of all to know who we are. What is the true nature of our humanity; what is the meaning of our selfhood?

In the last chapter we were saying that perhaps one reason we are reluctant to trust other people is that we cannot trust ourselves. We wear masks to keep our true feelings from being known by others, and, by the same token, we hide these feelings from ourselves. Also, if we are not to be blind to what virtue there is, the time must come when we trade our masks for mirrors in which we take an honest look at the reflection and remember what we see. This is part of what we see: by the very nature of our animal ancestry we enter life with organic hungers and biological urges—lust, fear, rage and hate—

which we often find difficult to hold in check and by which we are often embarrassed and ashamed; on the other side of our natures are hopes and dreams, godlike powers and aspirations after goodness and brotherliness and fellowship with God which we find difficult to achieve.

While this inner civil war is going on within us, we want the world to see us at our best and indeed we want to be our best and have a high opinion of ourselves. While we want others to think the best of us, we want to think the best of ourselves as well.

This is why we wear masks, but it is also why we must trade our masks for mirrors until we accept ourselves as we actually are.

II

The principle of self-acceptance comes first if we are to be ourselves. At this point, the trouble with many people is that they know their own faults and hate themselves for them, a circumstance which makes it impossible for them truly to love anyone else.

When they trade their masks for mirrors, they despise what they see. Instead of making peace with what they see, instead of accepting themselves for the good within them which should be encouraged and the evil which must be overcome, they despise themselves. Consequently, they find it impossible to trade their mirrors for windows that look out lovingly toward other people.

One erroneous assumption frequently made about the requirements of Christian faith in action is that while we feel we must describe in detail how one man ought to treat another, the same man can be expected to be spontaneously wise in dealing with himself. But anyone involved in counseling people who face all manner of problems soon discovers that underlying many of these problems is a tragic quality of self-hate. People need to be taught that it is quite as immoral to hate themselves as it is to be cruel and callous toward others. One's attitude toward himself can be psychologically just as complicated as his attitude toward others, and it is certain that until he loves himself properly he will find it impossible to love his neighbor as he ought.

We do not often give enough attention to this precondition of loving our neighbors. Jesus did, and the Hebrew tradition out of which He spoke did also. The command was simply "Thou shalt love thy neighbor **as thyself!**" A proper self image and self respect are essential to obedience to that commandment.

III

Self-acceptance is achieved and properly loving ourselves becomes reality when we look at our weaknesses and admit them; when we eliminate the picture of perfection, which we cannot achieve but which keeps us living with a sense of failure and inferiority to others; when, in short, we cease trying to be someone else and start being ourselves.

For nothing is more likely to create within us a sense of inferiority, along with the remorse and guilt which go with it, than an unswerving insistence on a perfection within ourselves which we cannot attain. The perfectionist is never satisfied with himself. As a businessman, he must be first in his field. As a professional he must be highly thought of. Socially he must have the biggest home, the largest salary, the most expensive car. The good qualities in other persons, other races, and other cultures usually escape his notice and his appreciation, despite the fact that, more than most people, he is governed by what others think of him. At whatever cost he must maintain the fiction of his perfection and superiority over those about him. He is never satisfied with himself and therefore he hates himself, a fact which spoils even the good he is able to do.

IV

But once he admits to himself and to his God that he is what he is and nothing more, then he makes important discoveries not only about himself but about God as well. To his amazement he discovers that God loves him with a love that will never let him go, that God loves him not because he is good and makes no mistakes but because God is truly God.

It is then that a man is released from the terrible burden of being perfect and is able to put aside all pretense and insecurity and false pride and give himself to making the most of what he is. A divine trust has been imposed upon us and we know it,but we also know that because we are finite and He is infinite, because He is loving and understanding and we are weak, our mistakes do not speak the last word, and our failures are not final. Therefore though we may be truly penitent concerning them, we are not overwhelmed by them. We do the best we can with what we have and are relieved of the awful necessity of making "a good impression" either on God or on our fellows.

In short we have been set free to accept ourselves for what we are, and in this freedom we find release to be ourselves. No longer must we act a part. No longer must we leave the right impression on others. We simply resolve to do the best we can with what we have, to accept the fact of our humanity and the consequences of it without fear. When we fail we know it is our fault; when we succeed we know that life has been good to us. In failure we make no alibis but look to ourselves to see why.

When the Dean Martin Golf Tournament at Tucson was shown on television Bobby Nichols was in the lead until the last few holes. On the 18th he still stood a chance. As he addressed the ball at the tee, a baby in the gallery began to cry. Nichols stepped away from the tee momentarily, then returned to hook his ball into a parallel water hazard on the left side of the fairway. His chance of winning had fallen into the water with that ball. Later when reporters tried to get him to blame that shot on the crying baby, he refused to do it. He simply said he should have had better control of himself—the baby and no one else in the gallery was to blame, only himself. That was the essence not only of good sportsmanship but of honest self-acceptance. When something goes wrong a healthy minded man will find out what it is and do what he can to correct it. He will assume personal responsibility for his bad shots which cost him the tournament as well as the good ones which permit him to win.

This is precisely what should take place in the larger game of life. We have to admit ourselves to be what we are, accepting our weaknesses as well as our strengths and determining to make the most of what we have.

We simply accept ourselves for what we are. We simply "be" ourselves and no one else. As Samuel Johnson once put it, "No man was ever great by imitation." He may be taught by others, but he cannot be what they are because he is himself and himself only.

This means a creative form of resignation to the limitations life has imposed upon us. When a man reaches that point he is able in utter honesty to say concerning himself, "Now I know what I have to work with. I wish it were more, but it is not, and with it I will do the best I can." And there is no way of reckoning where such resolution will come out.

The late Dr. M. E. Sadler had a personal motto by which he lived his very impressive and creative life. It was a motto allegedly written by Edward Everett Hale. It went like this:

> I am only one, but I am one.
> I cannot do everything,
>> but I can do something.
> I will not let what I cannot do
>> interfere with what I can do.

Well, some remember what a remarkable life was built upon that. It was a life of complete self-acceptance and self-reliance.

Ralph Waldo Emerson wrote: "There is a time in every man's education when he arrives at the conviction that envy is ignorance; that imitation is suicide; that he must take himself for better, for worse, as his portion; that though the wide universe is full of good, no kernel of nourishing corn can come to him but through his toil bestowed on that plot of ground which is given to him to till."

Surely that is what it means to accept yourself and be yourself and to love yourself properly so that you may then be prepared to love your neighbor as you ought.

do NOT feign affection

"Be yourself. Especially do not feign affection. Neither be cynical about love; for in the face of all aridity and disenchantment, it is as perennial as the grass."

When we come to this statement in the "Desiderata" we are brought once again to ideas made familiar to the Christian community by the Apostle Paul in the twelfth chapter of the Book of Romans.

"Do not feign affection. Neither be cynical about love," says the "Desiderata." "Let love be genuine," says Paul. "Hate what is evil; hold fast to what is good; love one another with brotherly affection."

The Phillips translation gives freshness to these verses from Romans: "Let us have no imitation Christian love. Let us have a genuine break with evil and a real devotion to good. Let us have real warm affection for one another as between brothers, and a willingness to let the other man have the credit."

"Do not feign affection!" In the Christian community **agape**—or Christian love—is a feeling of undiscourageable goodwill toward others which can exist even when you may not like the person who is the object of that goodwill. But in the Christian fellowship, Christian love is almost bound

55

to result in some degree of affection, of filial love, of love of the sort which has in it genuine feelings of identity with the person loved.

When Paul speaks of this "love" in the twelfth chapter of Romans he is talking about the kind of love within the Christian community which at its best does result in some degree of affection. Paul is saying in essence that this is a level of relationship between human beings which you do not play with or play at. It is either genuine or it does not exist. It does not have the quality of play-acting in it. It must be completely sincere. If it is an imitation Christian love, it is not love at all.

I

With all of this the "Desiderata" is in agreement: "Be yourself. Especially do not feign affection. Neither be cynical about love."

The reason these admonitions put such weight upon the necessity of genuineness with respect to love and affection is that love lies at the very heart of life's meaning; it is the focal point of the Christian Gospel both in its revelation of the nature of God and in its hope for the ultimate possibilities in human nature.

Because love is the central commitment of the Christian Gospel, it has the power to transform every type of human relationship. Gerald Cragg has observed that Christian love "takes up and enriches natural affection, so that the warm emotion characteristic of the family relationship at its best is brought into the family of God.''

Says he, "It expands and enlarges that narrow circle to which we usually restrict the action of our love and brings an ever wider area of human life within the scope of its power.

"But it also achieves the transmutation of a force which often works to destroy our peace and to poison human relationships. One of the marked features of our lives,'' says Dr. Cragg, "is the drive provided by the natural desire to excel. We crave superiority. In seeking to achieve pre-eminence we often embitter our own lives and those of others. . . . But in the Christian fellowship . . . the redirection of our craving to excel is manifested. We outdo one another in showing honor; each is quicker to recognize worth in and give recognition to others than he is to make claims on his own behalf.'' Love has the power completely to transform every type of human relationship.

This is so because, as Paul insisted, love is **the** quality which underlies the whole of God's redemptive activity. It is, as Dr. Cragg has observed, "the secret of all that God has done for us.''[1]

Love, then, is the one quality which, more than any other, must characterize the Christian community. For this very reason it must be absolutely without hypocrisy. Pretense is so antithetical to the nature of Christian love that the two cannot live together. Love is either genuine, without pretense, without hypocrisy, without imitation, or it does not exist.

II

This ought to be said: we live in a synthetic world where almost any good product can be imitated. We can buy across the counter a reproduction of almost anything we want, a fact which permits a working girl to wear jewels that look for the world like those which Queen Elizabeth wore in her coronation.

Some years ago when it was still thought that "cultured pearls were worn only by uncultured people" the Tecla Pearl firm ran the following ad in a national magazine. It was entitled "A $10,000.00 mistake":

"A client for whom we had copied a necklace of Oriental Pearls, seeing both necklaces before her said, 'Well, the resemblance is remarkable, but this is mine!' **Then she picked up ours!**"

You may be sure that ad sold a lot of pearls.

This art has not by any means been confined to the area of personal adornment. During World War II when we were cut off from the sources of supply of genuine rubber, the Allies rolled huge caravans of war material from one battlefield to another on synthetic rubber. To meet a critical need, scientists developed a process for making imitation rubber which might have spelled the difference between defeat and victory.

Indeed when you canvass the field of synthetic products, it will amaze you to discover to what extent the clothes we wear, the furniture with which we outfit our homes, the drugs and vitamins that help keep us alive are made of synthetic imitations of something else. They are, in some instances, better in the synthetic form than in the original, and far less costly.

III

This is not true, of course, of all imitations. Most of man's first efforts in this direction were for purposes of forgery, to get something for nothing, or at least for little.

It is when an imitation parades as something that it isn't that folk rebel against it. The danger of a counterfeit is that it brings the genuine under suspicion. Counterfeit money can wreck an economy if it is not detected. That is why during the War high American authorities voted against the proposal to drop counterfeit money all over Germany with the thought that the resultant inflation and confusion would wreck what was left of German economy before it could be detected. The proposal was turned down, according to one account, because it would have violated the ethics of war!

For purposes of forgery it is only the valuable and the costly that is reproduced, for these can be passed on to the unsuspecting as genuine. Against all such, wise and intelligent people must be on guard.

IV

While this is true of material goods, it is even

more important to be alert to counterfeit values, spurious ideas, imitation virtues.

This is supremely true of the principal virtue— Christian love. Says Paul, don't ever be a hypocrite with that. Says the "Desiderata," don't ever feign it, or fake it, or be cynical about it, for it is the one value we must not eliminate or dilute. Genuine love has some indispensable qualities and characteristics of its own which, if our life is to be good and meaningful, we cannot live without.

For one, it has the power to discriminate between that which is good and that which is evil. It is morally sensitive to the values of life, cleaving tenaciously to the good and making a genuine break with evil.

Genuine love can discriminate not only between what is good and what is evil, but also it has a remarkable capacity to discern the good possibilities in people and to bring into actuality "the things which it detects while they are merely possibilities."[2] Imitation love, a love that is faked, simply cannot do that.

Yet this fact about love is one of the major themes of the New Testament, continuously exemplified in the Gospels, particularly in the life of Jesus.

It would be unrealistic to assume that Jesus really did not know what the true condition of some of the people He dealt with actually was. Mary Magdalene was a woman of the streets almost wholly in the grip of evil forces. He knew that. But He also detected in her what almost everybody else failed to see, namely, the making of a saint! Zaccheus was a rascal who had sold out to the Roman Government as a tax collector among his own people, but Jesus recognized him as one to whom salvation might yet come. Probably few people even suspected such possibilities. In any event, a faked love would never have seen it.

Says Dr. Cragg: "Love alone possesses the power of discerning what is good and what is evil because love alone has the secret of the necessary insight. So far from being naïve and gullible, only love is free from the deceptions which mislead us in our judgments about men and movement."[3]

V

The "Desiderata" adds another word about it: "Neither be cynical about love; for in the face of all aridity and disenchantment, it is as perennial as the grass."

Of course! Those who are cynical about love never give it a chance to determine either what they do or how they judge other people. They look upon it as sheer sentimentalism when, in very truth, it is the essence of realism. So the "Desiderata" insists that we neither play the hypocrite about love on the one hand, nor be cynical about it when we view it in others. For in the face of everything that can go wrong, love lives on, it is the one perennial in life's garden of values.

You can neither be hypocritical about love when it is yourself you are thinking of, nor cynical about it when you discern it in others, cynical because you think they too are acting a part and are not genuine. You can do neither of these things and come out with the kind of love which holds life's profoundest secrets; because, only genuine love underlies the whole of God's redemptive activity in our behalf.

This is, indeed, the quality which must mark the Christian community if it is to be Christian.

You will find no better description of what genuine love really is than in Paul's letters to the Corinthians and to the Romans.

Genuine love, Paul insists, is love that is morally sensitive, cleaving tenaciously to the good and making a genuine break with evil, discerning the potentialities in others and doing what it can to bring them to the fore.

It is love which in humble self-effacement seeks to outdo one another in showing honor.

It is love which in unquenchable enthusiasm boils over, glowing in spirit.

It is love which is irrepressibly optimistic, full of joy, hope and patience, even "in tribulation."

It is love that draws upon the divine resources, being "constant in prayer."

It is love which causes men to sympathize with one another in brotherly affection, in every circumstance, rejoicing with those that rejoice and weeping with those that weep.

It is love which is never haughty or conceited, willingly giving itself to humble tasks. It is love that never avenges itself, but overcomes evil with good.

This is genuine Christian love as Paul describes it. And then he adds, as the "Desiderata" centuries

62

later did, do not feign love. Let us have no weak imitations of it. For only the real article, the genuine thing, can count. And the genuine thing which Paul describes is a set of fundamental principles delineating love in moral action. Love is not something about the Christian faith which you sit in a corner and contemplate. It is something to do. It is a set of attitudes that determine your relationship to yourself, to your God, and to your fellowman. It is the Way, the Truth, the Life.

What it does no imitation Christian love—no love that is faked—can possibly do. What it does no one who is cynical about it can possibly do.

For love is the very moral and spiritual grain of the universe. It hopes all things, believes all things, endures all things, and in the face of all aridity and disenchantment, it is as perennial as the grass.

NOTES

[1]**Interpreter's Bible,** IX, pp. 586-87.
[2]**Ibid.,** p. 587.
[3]**Ibid.**

TAKE kindly THE COUNSEL Of THE YEARS

In all the "Desiderata" there is probably no admonition more difficult to follow than this: "Take kindly the counsel of the years, gracefully surrendering the things of youth."

It is an admonition to grow old gracefully, to move from one period in one's chronological life to another, recognizing both the joys and inspirations of the new time and the things from the old which ought to be relinquished.

The Bible recognizes this necessity:

"Lord, thou hast been our dwelling place in all generations. Before the mountains were brought forth, or ever thou hadst formed the earth and the world, even from everlasting to everlasting thou art God. . . .A thousand years in thy sight are but as yesterday when it is past, or as a watch in the night. . . . .The years of our life are threescore and ten, or even by reason of strength, fourscore; yet their span is but toil and trouble; they are soon gone and we fly away. . . . So teach us to number our days that we may get a heart of wisdom."

Paul is even more emphatic: "When I was a child, I spoke like a child, I thought like a child, I reasoned like a child; when I became a man, I gave up childish ways."

"Take kindly the counsel of the years, gracefully surrendering the things of youth."

I

If we take kindly the counsel of the years, we will realize that it is the spiritual and emotional and not the chronological index in a man's life which is most important, so that if we advance chronologically and do not advance spiritually, gracefully relinquishing the things of youth, we are in for trouble. We rob our lives of both power and beauty when we do not see this.

Hardly anything is more pitiful to witness than a person growing into maturity but refusing gracefully to surrender the things of youth. And yet there are those who do just that. They grow old but they do not grow up. They refuse to release at least some of the things that properly belong to their younger years, forgetting that each stage in the advance of life has its own compensations. When the Psalmist wrote, "Teach us to number our days that we may apply our hearts unto wisdom," he was surely talking about the wisdom which recognizes the completeness of life at each of its levels and which requires a graceful surrender to the demands of time and a constant renewal of the values of the spirit which are the only abiding values.

Without such discipline a man or a woman presents the pathetic spectacle of refusing to be his age. One way or another, he will change, whether he

66

wishes to do so or not, and the change may be to his peril.

For as Charles Crowe has said, "The confidence of youth easily becomes the stubbornness of age. Ambitions unrealized can turn idealism into cynicism. The unreasonable accidents and tragedies of the years can harden into stone the gentlest hearts. Love loses its luster when it is undernourished. The once generous and unselfish soul can become petty and cantankerous. And faith in God and in life, when it is not renewed from day to day, dissolves into doubt and skepticism!"[1] For this cause the Psalmist cried, "Create in me a clean heart, O God, and renew a right spirit within me." Take kindly the counsel of the years, indeed.

II

The great need of our time is for people who do just that, who take kindly the counsel of the years; who become emotionally and mentally mature as they grow older; who are truly adult in their reactions to the emergent situations of everyday living, and who can, therefore, be entrusted with responsibility.

Some manage to do just this. If you become discouraged because of advancing years, remember that Immanuel Kant wrote his **Anthropology, Metaphysics of Ethics** and **Strife of the Faculties** at 74; that Tintoretto painted his "Paradise" and Giuseppe Verdi produced his masterpiece "Othello" in their mid-seventies; that at 80 Verdi produced

"Falstaff," and at 85 his "Ave Maria," "Stabat Mater," and "Te Deum." Lamarck at 78 completed his great zoological work, **The Natural History of the Invertebrates**. Oliver Wendell Holmes at 79 wrote **Over the Teacups**. Cato at 80 began the study of Greek, and Goethe completed his **Faust**. Alfred Lord Tennyson wrote "Crossing the Bar" at 83, and Titian at 98 painted his historic picture of the "Battle of Lepanto."[2]

All these were people who took kindly the counsel of the years. Instead of growing old, they gracefully surrendered the things of youth and grew up! They did not forget that true life is of the spirit and not of the flesh! They kept their minds and hearts growing with the years. They knew that, as Jesus said, life is more than meat and the body than raiment.

III

Now these remarkable people could not have done what they did had they not gracefully surrendered the things of youth and adjusted the pace of their lives to suit their changing needs.

Relinquishing the things of youth is no easy matter. Dr. Harry Emerson Fosdick once confessed that he was almost 50 years old before he quit using the phrase, "We of the younger generation." Of course he was no longer "of the younger generation," but few important lives lived in this century have reflected a greater capacity for taking kindly the counsel of the years than did his. On becoming a man, like Paul, he gave up childish things.

It is not easy to do. We enter this world wholly dependent upon the care of others, and without that care we would most certainly die. But, as we grow into adolescence, one of our major objectives is that of becoming independent. How many problems have unwise parents permitted to fret them because they did not accept the fact that the time must come when their children will be on their own and that if that time does not come, the child himself will not be taking kindly the counsel of the years.

Then the adolescent becomes a man and makes or would better make a new discovery about his relationship to his fellowmen. He can no longer be wholly dependent. He must stand on his own feet. Nor can he be wholly independent, for mutuality is at the heart of things.

Somehow the mature person who has taken kindly the counsel of the years and has gracefully surrendered the things of youth has found a synthesis. His dependence, as in infancy, was good but not good enough. His independence, as in adolescence he strove for, was good but was of itself not enough. Ultimately the synthesis of these two must be achieved: interdependence which gathers up the truth in dependence and the truth in independence into a living blend.

It is then that the mature person emerges. Paul recognized this truth. Every man shall bear his own burden, he says. This is independence. But one sentence farther on he says, "Bear ye one another's burdens and so fulfill the law of Christ!"

Law of Christ? Yes, His law—a cosmic law that

dependence is good but not enough, that independence is also good but not enough, that the
conscious blending of the two into a man who, insofar
as he can, bears his own burden, but recognizes, too,
that others are bearing a part of it, and who con-
sciously and willingly beyond his own dependence
goes out to bear the burdens of others!

IV

So do we surrender gracefully the things of youth,
and in the process we adjust the pace of life to suit our
changing needs. There can be no doubt that this is
what Paul meant when he said, "When I was a child, I
spoke like a child, I thought like a child, I reasoned
like a child; when I became a man I gave up childish
ways."

That was Paul's way of saying that one should
accept the mandate of his years, that we are to grow
up in our thinking, in our faith, in our actions, that the
effort to hang on to one's youth is to deny that
maturity brings its own opportunities and its own
responsibilities and satisfactions. It is these opportunities and satisfactions which we should
welcome with the advancing years, and adjust to
what they demand and require.

V

If we accept the mandate then we will remain

eager and enthusiastic participants in the wider sphere of life all about us.

There are areas of service which cry out for our help, and we remain vital persons by giving ourselves to them. There are opportunities of fellowship, in the church and beyond the church: literary organizations, musical groups, groups that meet just to play and enjoy life, groups that gather for creative work, other groups that meet for study and worship. Such activities are mushrooming over the nation and more and more people, as they grow older, are taking advantage of them.

What could be more important, if we are to take kindly the counsel of the years, than that we keep alert and sensitive to the larger currents and events of our time.

To live vitally and significantly in our day; to feel the winds of God in the sails of your life, however humble; to look out and see some of the great hopes of mankind being fulfilled in the world; above all, to see history as a sphere for the operation of God's will— that is what is required if we are to take kindly the counsel of the years.

It is to live on a new frontier. It is to realize that we live in an age of a thousand miracles, where space, time, and distance are no longer obstacles to our mobility, but where the great conquest yet to be made is the conquest of the inner man, and where the true meaning of life is achieved only by those who know that life itself is of the spirit and not of the flesh.

71

VI

In First Kings the story is recorded of the Lord's appearing to Solomon in a dream and telling him to ask for whatever he wanted. The event took place at Gibeon, where Solomon had gone to offer a sacrifice at the altar. Solomon responded to the offer with singular wisdom. Said he:

"Thou hast shown great and steadfast love to thy servant David my father . . . and now O Lord my God, thou hast made thy servant King in place of David my father, although I am but a little child: I do not know how to go out or come in. And thy servant is in the midst of thy people whom thou hast chosen, a great people, that cannot be numbered or counted for multitude. Give thy servant therefore an understanding mind to govern thy people, that I may discern between good and evil; for who is able to govern this thy great people?"

The prayer was pleasing to the Lord and God said to Solomon: "Because you have asked this, and have not asked for yourself long life or riches or the life of your enemies, but have asked for yourself understanding to discern what is right, behold, I now do according to your word. Behold I give you a wise and discerning mind . . . I give you also what you have not asked, both riches and honor . . . . And if you will walk in my ways, keeping my statutes and my commandments, as your father David walked, then I will lengthen your days." (I Kings 3: 5-15)

It was a wise and humble prayer and one that might well rise from every man's lips. The results sound very much like Jesus' promise, "Seek first the Kingdom of God and his righteousness and all these things will be added to you." For when we seek first of all from God and from life those values which ought to be first, our prayers are often answered more abundantly than we ask or think, as the years of our lives go by.

Take kindly the counsel of the years, gracefully surrendering the things of youth. Create in me a clean heart, O God, and renew a right spirit within me. So teach us to number our days that we may get us a heart of wisdom.

> Grow old along with me!
> The best is yet to be,
> The last of life, for which the first was made:
> Our times are in His hand
> Who saith, "A whole I planned,
> Youth shows but half; trust God; see all,
>   nor be afraid!"

Browning: "Rabbi Ben Ezra"

NOTES

[1]Charles M. Crowe, **Getting Help from the Bible** (New York: Harper and Brothers, 1957), pp. 50-51.
[2]From **Living Can Be Exciting** by Aaron N. Meckel Copyright © 1964 by Aaron Meckel and is used by permission.

seek spiritual strength for the unexpected

"Be yourself. Especially, do not feign affection. Neither be cynical about love; for in the face of all aridity and disenchantment, it is as perennial as the grass.

"Take kindly the counsel of the years, gracefully surrendering the things of youth. Nurture strength of spirit to shield you in sudden misfortune. But do not distress yourself with dark imaginings. Many fears are born of fatigue and loneliness. Beyond a wholesome discipline, be gentle with yourself."

"Nurture strength of spirit to shield you in sudden misfortune." That admonition, like most of the others in the "Desiderata," has the feeling and aura of a Biblical injunction. Where, more than in the Bible, is it made clear that spiritual strength for times of unpredictable misfortune is a cumulative thing, that the crisis does not create the character which can endure it, but only reveals what a man has been doing with his life in order to be ready for such an hour!

I

Once, a decade or so ago, a congregation heard a sermon inspired by the discovery that the Spanish

75

word for "battery" is **acumuladora**—a word derived from the Latin meaning to accumulate, or to store up power and energy to be called into service on demand. This is what a battery is, a reservoir of electricity, an energy bank, representing that margin of power, beyond what is in use, that will carry you through when heavier demands are made upon you. **Acumuladora!** A man's spiritual life should be equipped with precisely that ability. In how many ways can a man accumulate power for future use, laying it by in "storage" so that some day when having forgotten that he had it at all, he is able to draw upon it in a time of need.

II

This is what is always so amazing and so "miracle-seeming" about character at its best, the fact that people from whom you least expect greatness and who indeed least expect it from themselves, are always in a pinch demonstrating far greater capacities than they knew they had, great depths of being from which they are able to live and upon which, like exhaustless wells, they are able to draw!

Indeed, surely that is what character finally is. Character is not something you are born with. What you are born with may help or hinder, but at the last character roots itself in the reserves of spiritual quality which over the years you have been able to accumulate and which at any given moment you may be forced to levy some demand upon.

Great character, therefore, often seems unlikely in the forecast, simply because you don't know what, for any person, has been laid by in store. Don't ever be surprised then when you run into someone who demonstrates greater reserves than you knew he had. What a marvelous thing to see someone facing a bereavement that requires the complete re-organization of life, and doing it in such fashion that his own response leaves a benediction on everyone whose life he touches!

Or here is a person accepting a verdict about his own personal health—a verdict with which he will have to live out his life, accepting it with amazing serenity. Well, somewhere in that life, you may be sure, reserves were being laid away, character assets were being stored up, and now, when the load is laid upon him he has the power with which to stand beneath it.

There are folk, therefore, who remind us of the burning bush which Moses saw and wondered why it was not consumed. It was afire, according to the story, and it should have been burned to ashes, but it was not. Seeing a character like some of these we have been describing, like Moses we want to turn aside and see why the bush is not consumed.

III

Often when we find the answer to that question,

at the center will be the fact that repeated experiences of the worship of God have left a deposit of spiritual power in their lives.

There is a story to the effect that when George Matheson began going blind the girl he was engaged to broke the engagement because she did not want to marry a blind man. Matheson had every justification for becoming utterly despondent and embittered. Instead he wrote a hymn which we sing until this day, "O Love that will not let me go." Nurture strength of spirit to shield you in misfortune, indeed!

A man facing such a turn into the future alone and in the dark who still holds high his head and instead of weeping at his loss, sings for joy at what he has that still remains, and will remain forever, such a man has rooted his faith in acts of worship until he knows God face to face.

Sometimes we fail to reckon what happens to us in worship. We go to church Sunday after Sunday. We repeat the Lord's Prayer. We hear the sacred Scriptures read again and again. We go through the formalities of the Lord's Supper. And we listen with varying degrees of attentiveness to a sermon. How routine it may all seem in our less inspired moments.

Looked at from that standpoint, how formal and meaningless may it all become. There is danger there, to be sure, and no intelligent worshiper will discount it. But even so, what we cannot measure at all is the spiritual power that is being accumulated over the periods of time in these acts of worship when we commit ourselves week after week to those values apart from which life loses its sanctity. Even when we think we do not, we go away stronger than we came in. This is what the Psalmist meant when he said, "Wait on the Lord and He will strengthen thy soul!"

Nurture strength of spirit, indeed. Thank God for the spiritual reservoirs, filled over the years in the worship of God which provide us with the power we need when we need it.

This is the power which will enable Christian people in our community and throughout the land to find Christian answers to some of the problems that plague our culture. One reason why we should have no fear of the ultimate outcome of the crucial issues confronting us in these days in America is that by and large Americans are a worshiping people, and though here and there in the name of religion violent things may happen, in the long run as a nation we have spiritual reserves, and the spiritual commitments which will guide us into right courses. We will find the answers which will show respect and honor the dignity of all people and which will enable us without fear or shame to bow before the altar of Christ.

IV

Surely another contributing factor to our spiritual reserves is to be found in an experience which you would least suspect of being a source of power: the discipline of suffering. Leslie Weatherhead once said that many people ultimately find suffering to be a "frozen asset" which "later events unfreeze to their great enrichment and the confounding of their doubts." Weatherhead is right about that. For multitudes of people the discipline of suffering has turned out to be a source of spiritual wealth.

That was surely the case with Charles Dickens, who, as a boy, lived in a succession of shabby houses in an "atmosphere of sordid makeshift and continual debt." Ernest Tittle describes Dickens' father as done to the life as Mr. Micawber in **David Copperfield**. He was in and out of luck, in and out of debtor's prison, waiting for something to turn up.

"Prisoners for debt were permitted to see their families as often as they wished or the families wished. In fact, the wife and children of an imprisoned debtor sometimes moved in with him, having no other place to go. Mrs. Dickens once, when nothing was left, moved with the younger children into Marshalsea Prison, where her husband was confined. Charles, who had attained the ripe age of ten, was given a garret room outside, loaned to the family by some relative or friend, but he got his breakfast each morning in the prison. Yet even in this case such adversaries as lonely nights in a garret room and humiliating breakfasts in a debtors' prison were made to contribute to personal growth and achievement."

The experience did become a frozen spiritual asset which thawed out in Dickens' later life and became liquid in Nicholas Nickelby, Tiny Tim, Little Nell, Little Paul, Little Oliver, and "no little support for humanitarian movements that abolished England's debtor prisons and cleansed her schools of unspeakable barbarity."[1]

It is one of the most incredible things, when you ponder it, that suffering which all of us would like to avoid, but each of us must now and again endure, can itself be a source of spiritual power. I suppose that it is so because in the midst of suffering many a person has for the first time really found God because he has been driven to God.

Marty Mann, for example, was once a hopeless alcoholic. She is now a national worker in the field of alcoholism and a tremendous power for good. But years ago she was literally living in Hell as an alcoholic. But she says, "In the midst of my suffering I came to believe that there was a power greater than myself that could help me, to believe that because of that power, God, there was hope and help for me." So in the midst of suffering she found God, and in Him Power, power to rise above her own weakness into His strength, power to become a force for good instead of evil in the world.

This is the testimony which most truly great spiritual giants can bear: that what they have had to suffer, far from being a source of weakness, has time and again turned into a source of strength. One would suppose that this past generation never produced a greater spiritual giant than Harry Emerson Fosdick. Well, consider this autobiographical word which he wrote a few years ago:

"In my young manhood I had a critical nervous breakdown. It was the most terrifying wilderness I ever traveled through. I dreadfully wanted to commit suicide, but instead I made some of the most vital discoveries of my life. My little book, **The Meaning of Prayer,** would never have been written without that breakdown. I found God in a desert. Why is it that some of life's most revealing insights come to us not from life's loveliness but from life's difficulties. As a small boy said, 'Why are all the vitamins in spinach and not in ice cream where they ought to be?' I don't know. You will have to ask God that, but vitamins are in spinach, and God is in every wilderness.'' [2]

V

Another source of spiritual reserves is to be found in the personal disciplines which we place upon ourselves and which build up the reservoir of power.

It was the great psychologist and man of religion, William James, who once observed that if a young person will give himself to the disciplines of the career he has chosen for himself, staying with its requirements day in and day out, never giving up, then one bright morning he will wake up to the discovery that he is no longer a novice but an expert in his field! The only way one becomes an expert in any field is by yielding to the disciplines of it until he is able to do unconsciously, and with the artist's touch, what formerly he did by crude and studied effort.

All of this and more goes into the reserves of power which give to life the margin of depth which makes it worth the candle. Nurture strength of spirit, indeed. What an admonition to send us in a search of soul to see how we fare with our spiritual reserves! Here they are, disciplines which none of us can live well or greatly without: the discipline of work, the discipline of suffering, the discipline of worship, the discipline of self.

"Nurture strength of spirit to shield you in sudden misfortune. But do not distress yourself with dark imaginings. Many fears are born of fatigue and loneliness. Beyond a wholesome discipline, be gentle with yourself."

NOTES

[1]Ernest Fremont Tittle, **A Mighty Fortress** (New York: Harper and Brothers, 1950), pp. 14-15.

[2]Harry Emerson Fosdick, **What Is Vital in Religion** (New York: Harper Brothers, 1955), p. 9.

YOU ARE A CHILD OF THE UNIVERSE

"You are a child of the universe no less than the trees and the stars; you have a right to be here. And whether or not it is clear to you, no doubt the universe is unfolding as it should."

When Max Ehrmann wrote this sentence in the "Desiderata" in the first quarter of this century, the word "ecology" meant little if anything at all to the vast majority of people in the world. Within the past year or two you have probably heard more, read more, and witnessed more about "ecology," especially as it relates to the problem of pollution, than almost any subject other than the Vietnam War and the generation gap.

Ecology is defined as the science that deals with the mutual relationship between organisms, living things, and their environment. And the ecologist is concerned with that balance of nature in the environment best calculated to result in the well being of all living things.

I

What makes the issue current is that within the past decade or so we have become suddenly conscious of how mankind is polluting the soil on which he grows his provender, the air which he breathes and the water he drinks; how he is denuding the forests, placing great scars upon the face of the earth without attempting to heal them, and turning the living streams of water into streams of sludge and refuse. And this in turn confronts us not only with the scientific problem of sheer survival, but also with a problem which somehow must be faced prior to the scientific, namely, what is the role of man in his universe?

Is he, as the "Desiderata" says, a child of the universe no less than the trees and stars, or is he in some sense independent of it, in control of it, but not responsible for it? Is man nearer to the truth when he stands in awe of the universe or when he thinks of himself in terms of domination over it?

Both of these moods are sounded in the Eighth Psalm: "O Lord, our Lord, how excellent is thy name in all the earth. . . . When I consider thy heavens, the work of thy fingers, the moon and the stars which thou hast ordained, what is man that thou art mindful of him and the son of man that thou visitest him?"

There is the expression of awe and wonder and an admission that man is a child of the universe, no less than the trees and the stars.

But the Psalm ends with an affirmation which **can** mean the opposite of that, though it was probably not intended to do so. Listen: "Thou hast made him but little lower than God and hast crowned him with glory and honor. Thou has given him dominion over the works of thy hands, thou hast put all things under his feet—all sheep and oxen, and also the beasts of the field, the birds of the air and the fish of the sea and whatever passes along the paths of the sea. O Lord, our Lord, how excellent is thy name in all the earth!"

II

Which is he then? A child of the universe, interdependent with all its forms of life, or some near-angelic being who can do with nature what he wills to do, his dominion over the natural order meaning domination? Later we shall attempt to see the relationship between man as a child of the universe and man made in God's image and given dominion over the earth. But, for this moment, let us observe that in nature all living things appear to be interdependent with one another for sheer survival, and that whenever genuine imbalance occurs, all of nature seems to be affected by it.

Take, for example, this illustration from a lecture by Joseph Sittler.

"On the bank of a river that flows between high hills is a village. It has been there for centuries. The village has made an arrangement with the vernal and autumnal moods of the river: the houses and shops know how much the river rises with the spring runoff of the snow water and with the fullness of the autumn rains. Well up the bank they keep their distance.

"High in the forest-covered hills, too, a right relationship exists between trees and earth and forest animals and insects. By virtue of a marvelous ecological balance the life of each is regulated by the function of the others.

"Under the bark of the trees, for instance, there are millions of beetles which, undisturbed, would destroy the trees. But they do not destroy the trees because beetles are food for woodpeckers and the birds devour the beetles in such numbers as to keep the margin safe. On any summer's day . . . one can hear the birds about their happy ecological business! But one day a great beetle-infested tree so falls upon the soft-mounded earth that its underside is inaccessible to the birds. Thus protected, the beetles proliferate in the rotting timber. They spread from tree to tree now in such numbers that the bird-beetle balance is destroyed.

"Tree after tree is attacked, invaded, killed. The first ravaged acre increases to a dozen denuded hillsides. The billions of miles of earth-gripping hair roots die. When the rains come and the melting snow water gathers to a flood, the earth sponge, loosened now, nonfibrous and helpless, pours the water down the slope and with it the accumulated rich earth of unnumbered forest seasons. The old rhythm of the river is broken by a process that began with a strangely falling tree. The shops and houses at the river bank are flooded in the spring because the beetles on the far hills had an uninterrupted cycle of life."[1]

III

This story illustrates an inescapable fact of life: namely, its interdependence. As Rachel Carson once phrased it, "The history of life on earth has been a history of interaction between living things and their surroundings." And while the story illustrates what happens in the natural order without man's manipulation or interference, the fact remains that man is the only creature who has acquired significant power to alter the nature of his world.

And he is rapidly altering it. Says Rachel Carson, "During the past quarter century this power has not only increased to one of disturbing magnitude but it has changed in character. The most alarming of all man's assaults upon the environment is the contamination of air, earth, rivers and sea with dangerous and even lethal materials. This pollution is for the most part irrecoverable; the chain of evil it initiates not only in the world that must support life but in living tissues is for the most part irreversible."[2] And Miss Carson speaks of the pollution as a universal contamination of the environment. And this, not by the falling of a tree in a forest but as the result of the tremendous scientific and technological developments within the past few decades. But enough of this. You are surely aware of the results in smog in our industrial centers; the turning of our streams and rivers into sewage currents and the devastation of our forests. These are the results of the action of man. And man himself is part of the problem, for the population of the world is increasing faster than man's ability to increase agricultural production to match it.

IV

All of this means that the issue is not merely one of the scientific and technological knowledge, but of man's own understanding of nature and his own relation to it. That is first and foremost a theological matter. It is highly doubtful whether ecological

89

catastrophe can be avoided simply by applying to our problems more science and more technology. Real catastrophe can be avoided only by changing our understanding of the true nature of man in relation to his environment.

Some insist that man's abuse of nature has grown out of his religious conviction that nature is here primarily to serve man and for no other purpose; and that man's dominance which the Genesis account records is really not dominance in the sense of stewardship, but dominance in the sense of domination.

Which view is right we must leave to the experts. But this we know without a doubt: that man's current attitude toward the natural order and his relationship to it must undergo a significant change if man himself is not to die out of the universe as a result of his abuses.

For man has acted as though he were superior to nature, as if he were contemptuous of it and has been willing to use it for his slightest whim. In defense of the devastating commercial harvesting of the sequoia forests on the West Coast, a prominent politician is alleged to have remarked, "When you've seen one redwood tree you've seen them all." Is it possible that to a Christian man a tree is only a physical fact? Or is there some sense in which all living things are sacred because God has made them; and even though they are subject to man's use for his own survival, they are not to be abused or exploited as though they had no value except in terms of dollars and cents?

90

Whatever theologians have had to say about it, it does not follow, simply because the Genesis account urges man to be fruitful and multiply and to have dominion over all creation, that man was to abuse either of these privileges—either that of over-populating the earth or of exploiting wastefully the natural resources which sustain life upon this planet.

V

There is some evidence that there have been saints in the past who saw dominion as stewardship and all of life as something to be revered and not merely to be exploited.

St. Francis of Assisi is probably the greatest example from the Middle Ages. He was, at this point, a radical of the first magnitude. Lynn White has said that "The key to an understanding of St. Francis is his belief in the virtue of humility—not merely for the individual but for man as a species. Francis tried to depose man from his monarchy over creation and set up a democracy of all God's creatures. With him the ant is no longer simply a homily for the lazy, flames a sign of the thrust of the soul toward union with God: now they are Brother Ant and Sister Fire, praising the Creator in their own ways as Brother Man does in his."[3]

St. Francis preached to the birds because he believed there was something sacred in all the life God has created. In his own unique way he was rebelling against what man even in his time was

91

doing to nature and with it. He is regarded by some as the greatest spiritual revolutionary in Western history because he proposed an alternative view to the prevailing one regarding nature and man's relation to it: "He tried to substitute the idea of the equality of all creatures, including man, for man's limitless rule of creation. He failed."[4]

Whether man's having dominion over nature was meant to be unrestrained domination or reverent stewardship is no longer on logical grounds debatable. Unrestrained domination has brought us to the brink of disaster, and the roots of our trouble are essentially religious roots. Until we come to see and act upon the belief that St. Francis was in some profound sense correct, we are under threat. Someone has suggested that St. Francis be named the patron saint of the ecologists.

In modern times he had a counterpart in Albert Schweitzer, the great medical missionary, theologian and musician, whose philosophy of reverence for all of life would be a welcome message to the ecologists who are now so concerned with man's environment. According to the story, Schweitzer would not permit the killing of any animal except for food or unless the animal endangered human life, and even the life of insects he guarded against unwarranted destruction. As a medical man, but mostly as a devoted Christian, he took his position in full knowledge of the delicate balance which must be maintained in nature if living things are to continue living.

Frederick Elder in his meaningful book, **Crisis in Eden**, suggests that somehow we must in our time come to a new asceticism, not the old asceticism which denied the flesh as evil, but a new one which recognizes the value of human good in its relation to all the universe. Three words describe the new asceticism which he advocates: restraint, quality existence, and reverence for life.[5] The discipline of restraint would suggest restraint in the demand and acquisition of "things" which cause so much waste and pollution and restraint in the matter of human reproduction which would be a direct attack upon over-population.

An emphasis upon quality existence, instead of quantities of things, would bear upon this problem of pollution and destruction of natural resources. We have moved from a Puritan ideal of thrift into a state of conspicuous consumption, a course which somehow must be reversed. The new asceticism, as Elder contends, would not be world-denying, but life affirming, with a concern not only with what we acquire but with what we preserve as well. If what we really wanted were a better life rather than more goods and if we were willing to accept the discipline of it, it would make a significant difference in the manner in which multitudes of people in our affluent society live.

The third element in Elder's proposed asceticism is the Schweitzer principle of "reverence for all of life," which would put ethical considerations foremost in all of our decisions. [6]

We will have to come back to the simple admonition of the "Desiderata" to achieve this new asceticism: "You are a child of the universe no less than the trees and the stars; you have a right to be here." Accepting that simple principle you may go on to affirm as the "Desiderata" does, "And whether or not it is clear to you, no doubt the universe is unfolding as it should. Therefore be at peace with God."

NOTES

[1]Joseph Sittler, **The Ecology of Faith** (Philadelphia: Muhlenberg Press, 1961), pp. 3-4.

[2]Rachel Carson, **Silent Spring** (Boston: Houghton Mifflin Company, 1962), pp. 5-6.

[3]Lynn White "The Historical Roots of our Ecologic Crisis" in **Science,** Vol. 155, pp. 1203-1207, 10 March 1967. Copyright 1967 by the American Association for the Advancement of Science.

[4]**Ibid.,** p. 26.

[5]Frederick Elder, **Crisis in Eden** (New York: Abingdon Press, 1970), p. 145ff.

[6]**Ibid.,** p. 150.

bE AT pEACE

"You are a child of the universe no less than the trees and the stars; you have a right to be here. And whether or not it is clear to you, no doubt the universe is unfolding as it should. Therefore be at peace with God, whatever you conceive Him to be. And whatever your labors and aspirations, in the noisy confusion of life, keep peace in your soul. With all its sham, drudgery and broken dreams, it is still a beautiful world. Be cheerful. Strive to be happy."

The "Desiderata" begins with the admonition to go placidly amid the noise and haste and remember the peace there may be in silence. This is one kind of peace, the peace of tranquility and the contemplative heart. But the "Desiderata" goes a step farther and urges peace with one's fellows: "As far as possible, without surrender, be on good terms with all persons." This is the peace of good human relationships. Without it all other forms of peace are threatened.

But toward the end of the "Desiderata" are two other admonitions concerning peace. ". . . whether or not it is clear to you, no doubt the universe is unfolding as it should. Therefore be at peace with God . . . .whatever your labors and aspirations, in the noisy confusion of life, keep peace in your soul."

These are forms of peace denied those who have

not yet learned that they are not ultimately responsible for how the universe turns out.

In the last chapter we were speaking of man's "dominion over nature" as dominion which had more to do with stewardship than with exploitation. However good a case one may make that man is responsible for the uses which he makes of the material universe, the fact remains that the universe is God's; and while we have it within our power to deface, pollute and even destroy this world and the atmosphere about it, in the long run God reigns over all creation and over all history. The Christian man will do the best he can with what he has and encourage his fellows to do the same and leave the results in the hands of God.

On these two inseparable aspects of peace, so prominent in the "Desiderata" and in the Bible, let us think for a few moments.

I

". . . no doubt the universe is unfolding as it should. Therefore be at peace with God . . . . in the noisy confusion of life, keep peace in your soul."

How does one come by this, the profoundest need of the individual life?

Well let us begin by observing that the two are inseparable. Peace with God and peace within are two sides of one experience. If we gain the first, the second is its by-product.

As one searches the Scriptures and delves into

the deepest experiences of the saints who have stood in the Christian tradition, he may discern that there are several basic steps to attaining peace with God and peace within.

The first is obvious: to give yourself to God so completely that His rule in your life is not in competition with any other force in the world or with any god less than God.

We find peace with God when we accept God as the basic fact and factor in human life and history. In the "Desiderata" there is a qualifying phrase, and a good one. "Therefore be at peace with God, whatever you conceive Him to be ." And that "whatever" is an open door to continued growth in your understanding and knowledge of God. Every man has a right to pose his questions about God, but for the believing man the questions will have to do with God's meaning, His will and His purpose, and all such questions fall within the circumference of confident faith in God's reality. Really to find peace with God is to accept the fact that in His will is our peace and to learn to say, "Not my will but thine be done."

It was Thomas a Kempis who said, "For immediately you have given yourself unto God with all your heart, and have sought neither this nor that according to your own will and pleasure, but have together settled yourself in Him, you shall find yourself united and at peace, for nothing shall give you so gratifying delight as the good pleasure of the will of God."

Let there be no question, to keep peace with your own soul you must be at peace with God, and to be at peace with God is to find it in doing His will. William Law, a towering religious figure of the early 18th century, wrote in his **Serious Call to a Devout and Holy Life** that "If there is any peace and joy in doing any action according to the will of God, he that brings the most of his actions to this rule, does most of all increase the peace and joy of his life."

II

Of course this is true. The experience of multitudes of people through the ages bears witness to it. For the will of God has to do with day to day ethical and moral decisions, and there is no such thing as peace with God or peace within your own soul apart from fulfilling the ethical conditions of it.

To put it simply, a man cannot feel right unless he does right.

Somewhere along the line, if we are going to achieve for ourselves some center within that is serene and undisturbed, we will be obliged to quit fighting the claims of our higher selves. No man can feel right unless he does right!

This is a prescription for inward peace which for multitudes of people is not easy to take. We have been in recent years bludgeoned by the pseudo-psychologists who preach a gospel of relaxation as though Jesus had said, "Take up my cross and relax . . . Go into all the world and relax." But that is not what He said. A man with a guilty conscience cannot relax and for that very reason. His conscience ties him in knots.

An issue of **Time** magazine recorded the fact that the Liberian translation of the Lord's Prayer, by a misplaced inflection, has long had the Liberian Christians praying, instead of "Lead us not into temptation," "Do not catch us when we sin."

Well that would be a convenient escape, if we could arrange it. But it cannot be done. When we make evil choices, when we do wrong, it may be that no one else will know about it. You might even convince yourself that it has escaped the notice of God. But it will not escape your own conscience. For however poor our consciences are, they are nevertheless witnesses to the fact that we allow for a difference between right and wrong.

Our consciences testify to the existence of a moral universe where we cannot get by with what is essentially evil. The mercy of God may be infinite, indeed it is, but His demands are nevertheless inescapable. Do not catch us when we sin, my word! We never escape! Certainly one condition of peace with God and peace within ourselves is in Dante's famous phrase, "In His will is our peace," by which he meant at least this: that there are ethical considerations which must be met before any kind of peace at all is possible.

III

Consider two other conditions which must be taken into account if such peace is to be achieved.

One is certainly that we set our minds on what is

highest and best and, in the words of the "Desiderata," remember that with all its sham, drudgery, and broken dreams, it is still a beautiful world.

There is of course a lot of sham and drudgery and broken dreams. There is a lot of war and poverty and hatred in this world. We cannot escape it. We should do what we can about it. There is a lot of injustice in the world and we should do what we can to rectify it.

But any person who dwells constantly on what is wrong, what is evil and what is indecent and unfair in our world, even having done what he can about it, is calculated to have his emotional balance disturbed and even his mental equilibrium threatened.

It is not to be unrealistic occasionally to put the emphasis on the good, the true and beautiful in our world and affirm that with all its sham, drudgery and broken dreams there is much in which we can rejoice.

Paul did not consider it unrealistic or irrelevant to do this. He wrote his letter to the Philippians from a jail cell, and prison conditions in those days were horrible. Yet he says to his readers, "Rejoice in the Lord always; again I will say, Rejoice . . . Have no anxiety about anything, but in everything by prayer and supplication with thanksgiving let your requests be made known to God, and the peace of God which passes all understanding, will keep your hearts and your minds in Christ Jesus . . . . "

"Finally, brethren, whatever is true, whatever is honorable, whatever is just, whatever is pure, whatever is lovely, whatever is gracious, if there is any excellence, if there is anything worthy of praise, think about these things . . . and the God of peace will be with you!''

The only people who can meet this standard are those who, having done all they can about what is wrong with our world, quietly surrender their efforts to God in the conviction that the God who made this universe, and the God who needs our help in seeing that our portion of it is done right, nevertheless is the God who **runs** the universe and we can trust Him with ourselves and our loved ones in both life and death!

IV

If our peace is in His will, then it is His will that we become as St. Francis prayed, instruments of His peace. We do not leave everything to God. We leave only the results to Him, having done what we could, having done the best of things in the worst of times and hoped them in the most calamitious.

The prayer of St. Francis has become a part of classical Christian literature, for it expresses the kind of concern for goodwill and justice which the Christian must manifest toward all of God's creatures if he, himself, is to have any peace at all.

The prayer was St. Francis' way of saying not only that we must be identified with the other man's needs in order to find peace, but that we must get our own selves off our hands. Our preoccupation with our own selfish concerns must be taken out of the center of our interests before we can have a peaceful world, before we can have peace with God or peace with ourselves.

This is a day in which there is available unlimited opportunity for Christian action in meeting the vast and immeasurable needs in our world. We cannot wash our hands of those needs, however much at times we would like to do so. We must do what we can to bring a just peace to a war torn world; to bring economic justice to the underprivileged minorities in our own nation and in the world; and to help bear the burdens of suffering mankind, if we shall ever have peace with God or peace with ourselves. We must get ourselves and our selfish interests out of the center, and forgetting ourselves, take on "the burden of the world's divine regret."

Having done this, we can rejoice that with all its sham, drudgery and broken dreams, it is still a beautiful world. "Be cheerful. Strive to be happy." Here endeth the reading. Let us pray:

"O Lord, our Christ, may we have Thy mind and Thy spirit; make us instruments of Thy peace; where there is hatred, let us sow love; where there is injury, pardon; where there is discord, union; where there is doubt, faith; where there is despair, hope; where there is darkness, light, and where there is sadness, joy. O divine Master, grant that we may not so much seek to be consoled as to console; to be understood as to understand; to be loved, as to love; for it is in giving that we receive; it is in pardoning that we are pardoned, and it is in dying that we are born to eternal life." In Thy will is our peace. Amen.